Relax

A collection of short poems

By

Keith Hearn

Writing poetry is must like writing short stories

I hopefully my poetry will enable someone to connect with at least one poem

I hope to inspire others to write

Always follow your dream a dream will never disappear

Be Inspired

Never let others put you off

Be creative and enjoy the experience

A SUMMERS MORNING

Time to relax on a warm summer's morning,
Feeling the sun's rays on the skin

The last of the morning dew evaporating in the heat

The early morning bird song

Life feels so much better on a pleasant summers
morning

Life seems to pass by at a slower pace

The hustle and bustle of daily life is far away

CHANGE

I have finally accepted that my days with someone
has passed me by

It is time to stop looking and chasing

My effort is better harnessed in other areas

All I ever seem to do is to make a fool of myself

Maybe I have become too stuck in my ways and I
may not be able to change

Who knows?

BEER

How relaxing it is to sit with an ice cold pint of beer
on a summer's day

To sit and contemplate life and to think about what
is happening in the world

To sort the world out over a drink

Such a civilized way of sorting out the worlds woes

SPRING

Spring is in the air, everything looks new and bright

Flowers are starting to break out from their dark
tomb, the shoots are beginning to reach for the sky

The grass is turning a darker green

The trees are beginning to sprout their sweet
smelling blossom

The deer can be seen in the distance feeding on the
fresh succulent shoots on pastures new

DREAM

Everyone has dreams, not everyone follows their
dreams

I say never give up on your dreams

Dreams may not immediately come true

Stick with it and eventually it will come true

STREAM

The chalk stream is a pure and clear ribbon of water

Fish can be seen from the bank the fish dart from
one side to the other

The brown dappled colour on the fish's scales and
the odd bright glint of the sun reflecting on the
scales

The river meanders into the distance

The gurgling of the water can be heard as it passes
over the shingle on the river bed

It is such an idyllic and beautiful scene

THE END TO DARK NIGHTS

For months the night and days have been so
depressingly dark and cold

The routine of going to sleep in the dark and waking
up to the dark during cold mornings is beginning to
fade

The days would drag, as the hours and minutes
slowly ticked away

All of a sudden the days have become brighter and
warmer

It feels so nice to get out of bed in the mornings.

The morning light making the start of the day so
much more bearable

The world seems so much easier to face on a warm
summers morning

KINDNESS

Who knows what someone is about?

How they will react, some people cannot handle
kindness

Some people are very suspicious of people who are
kind

Many have only known unkindness in their lives

The opposite can have the same affect

TWO

Two is such a big number

It takes two to share the ups and downs of life

Sharing is a distant memory for me

I seem to have cut myself off from others

I have to learn to let someone back into my life

I need to start to pull the barricades down no matter
how long it takes

RELAX

THE SUN

The sun warms up so many hearts

It is an inspiring force in the world

It inspires all of us to think and feel good
about ourselves and others

13

KEVIN

A very kind lady with lots of affection

I could tell straight away that you are kind hearted

You would always put your hand on my arm which meant a lot

Even though you were always busy, you found the time to talk

It was so funny when you introduced "Kevin"

How I laughed once I realized that Kevin is your dog

Indoors he loved running up and down

He was a ball of fur until he was sheared

RELAX

Whenever you were at work you had your hair up in
a bun

Until one day you had your hair down, I realized
just how pretty you look

THE DOG

I watched as the lady held her baby in her arms

I could see another lady sat with her

It seemed as though she too was talking to a baby in
a pushchair

Oh how I laughed when she picked up her dog from
the floor

It was so comical

COPING

We all need somebody in our lives

I thought that I could cope living on my own, I have
since found that it is not the case

As I hurtle towards the latter stage of my life

All of a sudden you appear in my life

My life has gone through many twists and turns

I sometimes feel that I don't deserve your love

My life will blossom with you

I feel that my life will be complete with you in it

LONGING

I can see you whenever I want to and you never
complain or make a fuss

My eyes look at you from a distance

You stand there with so much pose and authority

Your eyes are so sharp and alive

How I long to be with you
To hold you close and to tell you how I feel for you

TIME

It felt so good to have a cuddle with you

It was the last thing that I was expecting

It made me realise what I am missing

The love and contact of another person in my life

The good things in life take time

It is well worth the wait

UNDERSTANDING

I sometimes do not understand you, I do not know
what is going on in your head

Would I want to know what is going on?

That is the question

I am sure that you are a lovely person, it is just that
I do not know where this is leading to?

Sometimes my head feels as though it has gone
through a washing machine, on a full spin

THE AUSTRIAN LADY

This is to the lady who has come from a land of
plenty, in Austria or is that Australia

Her English humour is spot on

Such a wonderful lady, who always has a smile

It is Austria's gain that she is going back home

Our loss

BRIGHTNESS

A bright room will always make anyone feel good
first thing in the morning

The sun lighting up every room in the house

I feel so enlightened ready to take on the world

To grab the world with both hands

Enthused to make the best of the day

VILLAGE LIFE

Things are quiet around the village

The sun is out and the birds are in full song

It is the first day of spring

People seem to be in a good mood and look happy

Life feels so good

Who knows what may happen when days feel like
this

I feel lucky to live in such an inspirational place

ALL GOOD THINGS COME TO AN END

I never thought that things would end this way

I thought that I had found someone to call a soul mate

You always knew how to keep me interested in you

I think a break from one another is a healthy thing to do

The situation that we found ourselves in was not concussive to a healthy relationship

ROLLING FIELDS

The rolling fields spread out before me in a
spectacular panoramic view

Bale upon bale of hay are neatly rolled in rows

Hawks are hovering above the field

Buzzards are souring high in the sky riding on the
thermals, suddenly swooping down into the freshly
cut field

Diving onto unsuspecting voles and mice

From a distance the fields look so peaceful but
above and in the fields there is a battle for life

ONE DAY

One day are a few words that flash across my mind
time and time again

One day things will get better, it is something that
we all strive for in our lives

To stay focused on a dream

Who knows what will happen

Whatever our goal is

"One Day"

EASTERN PROMISE

As I look up from the page of my book, I observe
what is happening around me

People are getting on with their business

Across from me I notice a pretty blonde lady

She is brimming with confidence, she has the look
of an eastern European possibly Russian

She is having lunch with an elderly gentleman

As she stood up and left the table she walked with
such elegance

It is so hard not to notice that she has a pretty face,
it was also noticeable that she was older than she
looked

Not because she was wearing makeup, as she
wasn't wearing any, as she did not need makeup

A SLOW PACE

Life seems so slow

I am not built for speed

All I need is a nice damp cold day

I thrive in the damp

I get used to the weight on my back

I leave a trail of a sticky substance wherever I have been

I sometimes get attacked from above, I never see my attacker as they attack from a great height

I carry my house on my back

I love my life as a snail

MOVEMENT

Bushes, trees and fields are rushing by
Leaving that precise moment frozen in time
Everything disappears in a flash

Clickety clack the sounds of the train's wheels on
the rail track, clickety clack

Whoosh the swaying feeling as the train passes
another train

The train travels over rivers leaving a blue streak on
the mind

Houses and fields are a blur as the train passes
through villages and cities leaving them in its wake

Clickety clack, whoosh everything is a flash as the
train eats up the track in seconds

BUTTERFLY

You are so much like a butterfly that has been
encased in a cocoon for so long

Only now you have been released from a world
without love and affection

You are a beautiful creature and have the rest of
your life to live and breathe

Such a beautiful creature is meant to fly and dance
in the sky

Not to be hidden away from the world

THE STARS

Is it time to stop looking up at the stars on a cold
winter's night?

Time and time again on a cold winter's night
making a wish, wishing for the thing that others
take for granted

The last time that I had something that I had wished
for I let it slip through my fingers

I let it go far too cheaply

I know how costly it is to have a wish taken away

TRAVELLING

As the train drew up to the platform

The sunlight was beginning to break through the city skyline

The sunlight is breaking as the city comes to life

How nice and peaceful it seems on the platform

Everybody ready to start a journey into the unknown

People trying to find the carriage door to get a seat on the train

The train waits at the station disgorging its human cargo

Waiting for the next batch of human cargo

RELAX

Once the train has had its fill it begins to move out
of the station

Initially it moves off gently at first it suddenly
builds up more speed and power

Until it is a distant object at the end of the station

THE RACE

Fly, fly faster you can catch up
You can do it

Flap, flap your wings harder
The bird's wings are flapping so hard
The bird's eyes are almost popping out of its head

Hedgerows are flying past the train's window
Fields are a blur merging into one colour

Alas the bird is left behind a tiny blob in the
distance

Such a valiant effort to overtake the train

A distraction during my train journey

THE YELLOW FIELD

In the distance the green field becomes bright
yellow

As the sun burns high in the summer's sky
The yellow field takes on a shine

How bright the field looks from a distance

The field stands out like an oasis in a desert
Amongst the green fields

Trees naturally frame the yellow field amongst the
surrounding fields

THE WALK

As we walk, the night closes in
Walking along a broad avenue towards Penny Lane

The old lady found it difficult to keep up
She was being helped along by her granddaughter
and grandson

She asks "how much further do we have to go"?

On either side of the road, derelict houses and
boarded up shops looked so forlorn

The rubbish was blowing everywhere, like the
bushes in a Wild West film

The surrounding area looked deserted

RELAX

The old lady shouted "who would want a birthday
"do" in a dump like this"

She was only saying what everyone was thinking
but did not want to say

NIGHT TIME

The night time and what all of its connotations
evoke in most people

All is so very quiet and peaceful
No one to disturb ones thoughts

It is just a façade night time is the time that one's
imagination run riot

Our out of control thoughts take control of our
thoughts

During the night, the noises and sounds that are
unheard of during the day, they creep into ones
imagination

Every sound comes alive

It is as though the house is alive

RELAX

What a wonderful but scary time of day
Imagination's running riot

IN THE GROUND

Deep in the ground it is so cold

There is no sunlight
All I do is sleep all day in the dark

When I am awake my energy is used up for
searching the light

As spring arrives my efforts are rewarded

My shoots break the surface of the soil

How wonderful it feels to break into the sun

The energy from the sun is taken down to my roots
working so hard deep in the soil

In the summer my flowers are in full bloom in
various bright colours

RELAX

I help the butterflies and bees feed on my nectar

Until autumn and winter once again sets in

The cycle is repeated

I hate the cold and the dark, I cannot wait for spring
to arrive

FLU

How the flu has a lot to answer for

Not just falling ill

It was during a severe bout of flu that I realised that
I don't like my own company

When someone is ill and alone, it soon kicks in, not
being able to share the little things in life, the
everyday things

It is why I say that it is not just about catching the
flu bug

I thank my last bout of flu for making me realise
what I am missing

THE END OF WINTER

As the first of the suns rays pierce through the grey
winter's sky

The sun makes everyone feel so good, after the
many months during the darkness of winter

More and more the birds are arriving in the garden

A spring morning is such a heartwarming sight

The various spring bulbs are pushing up the shoots
through the cold soil

Spring has finally arrived in all its splendor

The garden will borders will be covered in a carpet
of colour

DREAMERS

We can all follow a dream, a dream that may have
been formulated as a child

As we become older that dream may fade

Always follow the dream, no matter how faded it
may become

The dream may change one's life forever

MONEY

My life or my view on life? Maybe for some, be
seen as naïve

I see the good in everyone

We live in a very greedy and grasping world

A world of profit and greed that leaves others
behind

It is a world of people squeezing every penny out of
others

SPACE

To be able to see the earth from space in pictures is such a revelation

To be able to see the earths beauty is amazing

There are also the pictures of the devastation of earth's bounty

It must be awe inspiring to be one of the lucky few astronauts to be housed on the space station

Looking across the earth and looking out into the vastness of space

TIME AND TIME AGAIN

Why do we come back to the same person time and time again?

We do it even when we know that it will end in tears

We are all creatures of habit

TALKING

How pretty she looks talking to a friend

She mentions how she and her boyfriend are not getting on and how heartbroken she feels about the situation

She continues and explains that their relationship is rapidly going down the pan

The world seems a lonely place when dreams crumble, wither and die

A COLD WINTERS MORNING

With the frost on the ground and the cold morning
air freezing turning breathe into plumes of hot air

Feet and hands are so cold

The trees and bushes holding a spiders web in a
frozen grip

All around there is a white coating just like icing
sugar covering everything

It is nice to take in the spectacle of a typical
winter's scene

It reminds me of the winters as a child

"BRING ME SUNSHINE"

The couple looked so happy on their special day

They had their favorite music playing in the background

It was their "big day" their wedding day

Invited guests looked so pleased for the couple, who in a few minutes would be married

As they walked up the aisle, after the ceremony was completed, the bride and groom broke into a dance

They could not stop smiling and grinning just like a Cheshire cat

They danced the "ship dance" bring me sunshine

They were so happy on their big day

PASSING BY

Do you ever feel that life is passing by leaving you
in its wake?

Sometimes I have to slow down and stop chasing
time

I believe I should I stop and start acting my age?

My body is old my mind remains in a younger
vortex

I feel that I have much left to do, I feel that I have
not yet reached my goal

I push myself to the limit, trying to halt time

Old age will eventually catch up with me

Until then I will be the age I want to be

ADOPT THAT STANCE

He stands with his wife deep in conversation

He is engrossed in the conversation

His wife suddenly indicates that he is getting
frustrated and that he will adopt his normal stance

All of sudden he places one of his hands onto his
hip

Oh how funny he looks, his wife and others burst
into laughter

He soon realizes what he has done

He finds the humour and bursts out laughing

SUMMER HOLIDAY

Where shall the family go on holiday this year?

It is a question a lot of families will be asking this year

The world has changed so much

The innocence of the world has evaporated

Some areas of the world are off limits and far too dangerous to take a family on holiday

I suppose it will have to be a local holiday this year

Let's hope that the British weather makes an appearance this summer

HARD WORK

Anyone can follow their dream it only needs a large
dollop of faith and hard work

MEMORIES

How amazing it would be if in the future, our
memories can be saved

To be able to download our memories from birth or
later in life

I would like to be able to view my memories, it
would be so fascinating

To capture the past and see how the past has shaped
our future just like a movie

EXPERIENCES

During my military service there was a mixture of
humour, laughter and sadness

There are memories that have seared themselves
into my conscious

The ones that spring to mind are the good memories

The sad times are soon forgotten, to be locked away
in the dark recesses of my mind

Over time the sad memories fade

MISTAKES

We all make mistakes at some time in our lives

I seem to miss-read or misunderstand the fairer sex

I saw her for the first time close to her car

I thought that she was visiting a friend, she looked
so pretty

To my hearts delight I found that she was living
close by

I was smitten, how horribly wrong I was about her

I have certainly learnt one thing, I am not too old to
make mistakes

COLOURS

I realized as I stood with you the greyness inside of
me had suddenly changed to the vibrant colours of a
rainbow

When you left I thought "what the hell has
happened to me"

The feelings had totally taken me by surprise

It felt as though someone had opened a door to my
heart

I want the door to remain open

THE TREADMILL OF LIFE

I could see my dream in the distance it seemed so
far away

Each time I get closer to fulfilling my dream, it
seems to move further away

It was as though I am on a treadmill seemingly
going nowhere very quickly

Some people manage to get off the treadmill to
reach their dream

I feel that I am still on the treadmill

Will I ever reach my dream?

RED

Early morning at the railway station, people arriving
for the early train they look very tired and harassed

People arrive at the same time day after day

When I first waited for the train I thought to myself
do I really want to do this every working day?

There was one person who stood out from the
crowd from those who wear, a uniform of the same
black and grey clothing

It was a lady who wore a bright red coat
She would laugh to herself as she watched
something on her electronic device

She always looked very smart and wore a red coat

MY WORLD

Dreams, all of the years attending school, who would have thought that I would turn to writing in later life?

Constantly being sent out of lessons to be shoved into an empty classroom to stare out of a very large window

To watch others outside going about their business

Not being able to join in with the rest of my class

It was during this time that I switched to watching others, to observe what others were doing

It enabled me to observe others mannerisms
I had the time to look out of "my" window

I may have thought at the time that it was a waste of time

RELAX

Later in life I believe that it was time well spent, it
has helped me to have such a vivid imagination

To dream of things to write about

All was not lost I did not realise it at the time

WINTERS SLUMBER

Spring is such a turning point in nature

It is the time when nature begins to wake up from
the winter slumber

The weather starts to change for the better

The sun breaks through and makes spring look so
bright

The daylight breaks through earlier

People as well as nature feel so much better during
this time of year

WHO ARE YOU!

Others see you as a mother and wife the person who
runs after others

Who is looking after you?

You automatically respond to "what's for tea, where
my shoes, is the water hot and have you been to the
shops?"

When at work you feel that you are also taken for
granted, others push you to the limit

I can hear the scream from within "please look at
me I am here"

There is another you trying to escape the drudgery,
a person no one has yet seen

Look no further if you really want someone to take
you away from the daily grind

SNOW

Snow as it covers the landscape is such a beautiful
sight

Many look forward to waking up on a winter's
morning to see the spectacle of a cold frosty
morning

Snow is created in such a complicated manner

The flakes of crystalline water ice that falls from the
clouds

As it covers the land and creates a blanket of snow
it also creates a winter wonderland

TOUCH

Touching one another, is such a natural action both for humans and animals

It shows so much affection

It arouses so many senses

It may arouse senses that have lain dormant for so long

Sometimes touch is the action that may comfort someone who is ill

The sense of holding someone is something that should never be taken for granted

THE WIND

I see her walking past my office every day

I notice how the wind whistles trough her hair

It is the small things that I notice about you

It is times like this that I appreciate you for letting
me into your world

PAIN

The pain has been so great that it has been eating
away at me from within

The pain has had such a bearing on my life

It has masked so many aspects of my life

Time has proved to heal the festering sore

The pain is still deep within, for so long I have
hidden it so deep

The pain no longer rules my life

I now rule the pain

SHARING

Today has been a wakeup call

It is time to share my life with someone who wants
to share their life with me

Sharing with someone that you love is such an easy
thing to do and at the same time the most difficult
thing

DEEP DOWN

Deep in your heart is there room for me?

Is there a place for me?

I have so much room for you

DEER

On an early foggy morning I look across the field

With the mist swirling in the breeze the scene could
have been the same as our ancient ancestors may
have come across

Deer appeared from the safety of the woods

They are grazing in the field on the fresh grass as
the sun is starting to break through the mist

The scene is mystical and ancient this is the
countryside in its glory

This scene has never changed for millennia

BARGAIN

How people run around scurrying in the shop
looking for bargains pushing one another before the
shop runs out of bargains

How they remind me of squirrels searching for nuts
to bury for later

People morph into totally different people as they
try to grab a bargain

Their personalities totally change to nasty and
aggressive hunters

Some fight and bite or shout at one another, to
spend their money on a so called bargain, what they
think it is a bargain

Others may think it just isn't worth the hassle for a
so called "bargain"

DECADES

My life feels it is slowly changing for the better, it
has taken decades to arrive at this point

Who could have known when I was a child that I
would be writing books for the world to read

My school life was not the best in the world

I felt as though I was cut adrift from the main
teaching process

I had one thing that never left me, my dreams

Only decades later I have begun to turn my dreams
into reality

Never let go of your dreams

JUST ME

I realise that I do not make sense to everyone that is
just me

I can come across to others as a little eccentric that
is me

I can say the most oddest of things, that is just me

I can come across as a person that likes my own
company that is just me

I am the most pleasant and kind person, that is just
me

I fall in love so quickly, that is just me

I have so much to give the right person that is just
me

THE VILLAGE PUB

The sound of clinking glasses greats the customers
as they enter the bar

The crash of cutlery being cleaned and placed in the
container resound in the air

The music is gently playing in the background

The sound of people chatting as they eat

It is such a busy place it is also a relaxed place to
visit

People are smiling and laughing

It is a warm and a welcoming place to visit

For others it can be a sad place

ROBIN

The Robin waits for me to dig another part of the
garden waiting for its next meal

As I turn over a spade of soil then move to the
another section of the garden the Robin begins to
dig the soil with its sharp beak turning over the soil

Suddenly it lunges for a worm in the soil

The worm is not quick enough and the Robin has
the worm securely in its beak it flies off with its
meal into the nearest bush

There is much chirping from the Robin informing
its mate that it has a fresh meal

CRYING

You send your messages for all to see on social
media

Sometimes your messages are sent with no
explanation

Is it a cry for help?

You make out that you are one of the "boys" a
woman who can take the male banter

I sometimes think that it is just a front and that
some of the comments may cut you to the bone

You really do need someone in your life someone
who you can rely on and not to use you and drop
you like a sack of potatoes

Your silence speaks volumes

RELAX

THE PAST

I sometimes wonder how we ever made it.

Things were difficult for the children

I don't think that I could have survived if I was in their position

It was such an emotional time

Their lives were turned upside down
Their parents in a feud that has lasted for decades

What could I do?

The only thing I could do was give them love and to remain by their side

HUMBLE BEGINNINGS

I very often think about how far we have come as a
family

The things that we have seen and done during our
lives

Our playground as children was within a war zone

How lucky we have been since then

Working in most of the war zones in this and the
last century

This has been a positive thing rather than a negative
time in our lives

COUNTRYSIDE

Take time to see the countryside

If you do it will open up the mind

It costs nothing to walk in the countryside and
observe nature in its natural habitat

A gift from the heavens

VOICE

I can hear a voice in the distance

The sound of her voice reminds me of licorice

It is so thick and sweet

Her voice isn't hoarse or loud it is deep and thick

Just like licorice

HOW GOOD DOES IT FEEL

How good does it feel to come to the end of a project?

For me it is the best feeling

To know that others will see the fruits of my work

After weeks and months of hard work the fruits of my efforts are there for all to see

To know that I have finished the work it is so fulfilling

It makes me feel so good

THE WICKED TWIN

How pretty she looks

I am not sure how she takes my sense of humour

She teases me with her inner wicked twin

How much I look forward to meeting her wicked,
naughty twin

No one would ever think that she had a wicked side

FOOTBALL

The ups and downs of a football supporter

To see your favorite team go two nil down within
twelve minutes

It is soul destroying, there is always hope that your
team can claw something out of the seeming defeat

Your team suddenly scores a goal they have handed
given you hope

All of a sudden it is three on, once again your heart
sinks

And then it is the fightback your team scores yet
another goal and it is three two

Your living room is electric the TV blaring away
the commentator is hysterical

RELAX

See your team manager encouraging the crowd to
get behind the team

Oh my lord your team draw level

You think here we go extra time

But no your team scores a fourth goal

The stadium rocks the home crowd go wild
The manager has lost it he is dancing up and down
the touchline screaming and shouting

The sound of the final whistle
We have won

Once you have calmed down it is time to tidy the
living room, it looks like a bomb has hit it

Once again Liverpool have added to the football
history that is Anfield

98231210R00048